WHAT PEOPLE ARE SAYING ABOUT FROM THE DUST

"**The moment** my kids saw it they **loved it**... My cousin commented on how nice it was that they were **playing 'Book of Mormon' rather than Transformers**...!"

— *Heather Farrell*
womeninthescriptures.blogspot.com

"*From the Dust* comics are **way cool** and also **full of scholarship** to back them up. I was impressed. If you have young boys (or super cool girls) these might **rock your world**. Your grown up boy might like it, too. (**I got one signed for Rocky**, my soon to be **husband**!)"

— *Felice Austin*
co-author, The Gift of Giving Life

"I **was fascinated** by the **presentation** and the **boldness** of his vision...Kudos to Mercer for stepping out and making this bold move into the Mormon publishing world. Only time will tell if he succeeds. **I hope he does**. He has **something to say**, and an entirely **creative way of saying it**. Please, give the web site a look, and enjoy this foray into creative Mormonism."

— *Jeffrey Needles*
The Association for Mormon Letters

"Your project has inspired me...Your **focus on education** and **exposure to both scripture** and **art-making** makes your ideas stand out. I have seen other Book of Mormon subjects **come and go** but I think **your project is a keeper!**"

— *Micah Clegg*
smokinpencil.com

Springville, UT, USA

FROM THE DUST #1: THE LAST KING OF JUDAH. Published by SPIDER COMICS and produced by ZADIK PRODUCTIONS. © 2013 Michael Mercer. All rights reserved. *From the Dust* is a work of fiction. It in no way represents the official views of any religion or organization. All characters in this issue, their distinctive personalities, names, and likenesses are trademarks of Michael Mercer. No similarity between any of the names, characters, persons, and/or institutions in *From the Dust* with those of any living or dead person or institution is intended, except in the case of historical figures from the Hebrew Bible or the Book of Mormon which are in the public domain. Any such similarity which may exist to any other person or entity is purely coincidental. This includes other works of fiction. Spider Comics and its logos are ™ and © Spider Comics 2012. The *From the Dust* logo and its variants are ™ and © Michael Mercer, 2013. All other content is © Spider Comics, 2013. For more information email info@spidercomics.com or visit www.spidercomics.com or www.bookofmormoncomic.com. PRINTED IN THE USA. For business production inquiries for games, videos, and more please visit www.zadikproductions.com.

From the Dust

The Story of the Hebrew Bible

#1

— The Last King of Judah —

Contents

Introduction	6
The Series	14
The Cast	17
The World	38
The Story	52
Scriptures	72
Hebrew	82
Sketchbook	87
Next Issue	92
Sneak Peek	96

Written & Illustrated by
Michael Mercer

— WWW.BOOKOFMORMONCOMIC.COM —

כִּי־עָפָר אַתָּה
For dust thou art...

...and unto dust shalt thou return.
וְאֶל־עָפָר תָּשׁוּב׃

CREDITS

Acknowledgments

The publisher and producers would like to thank the following for their extraordinary support and contributions to this project:

Michael Mercer

Matt & Maria Adams, Aaron Mercer, Adam Mercer, Al Domeshek, Josh Metcalf, Dave Buer, Mike Jones, Alan Hickey, George Johnson, Rulon Osmond,

Brent Adams

Ryan Woodward, Kelly Loosli, Cynthia Hogan, Richard Schmid, Jason Kim, Catherine Ganiere, Jake Parker, Tyler Carter

Benjamin & Elise Swank, James Cook, Matt & Camie Webb, Jennifer Tays, Hailey Toro, and Natalie Shaw.

Michael Mercer would like to show especial thanks to his family, in particular his parents, for their generous support of *From the Dust* since its inception. *From the Dust #1: The Last King of Judah* is dedicated to them, with gratitude.

Artwork

All artwork in *From the Dust #1: The Last King of Judah* is created by Michael Mercer under the direction of Spider Comics.

Copyright

All rights reserved. Published by Spider Comics. No part of this book may be reproduced or transmitted in any form or by any means, eletronic or mechanical, including photocopying, recording, or by any information storage and retrieval system, without written permission from the publisher. All artwork copyright Spider Comics.

For information address Spider Comics,

P.O. Box 71, Springville, UT, 84663-0071

Produced by Zadik Productions, LLC

www.zadikproductions.com

ISBN 978-0-9859884-1-8

INTRODUCTION

THE BIGGEST STORY
Never Told

> " *There is no greater agony than bearing an untold story inside you.* "
>
> — Maya Angelou

Would you believe me if I told you that the biggest story in all of scripture is also one that you have never heard? As far-fetched as this claim may sound, it is, in fact, astonishingly true.

Deep inside the Old Testament there is a story that has been waiting to be told for a very, very long time. This story, although virtually unknown to most of us, is at the heart of the entire book. It is the story that both *started* it all in one way and *ended* it in another.

It begins in the first chapters of Genesis, but it is not the creation story. Its themes are woven into the tapestry of nearly every book in the Old Testament. At the climax of this story it prophesies that it will

Jeremiah visits Euphrates. See Jeremiah 13:1-11.

become equally significant to the Hebrew people as the story of the Exodus. Indeed, Moses concludes his writings prophesying of the day when this important, but mysteriously unknown, tale would occur.

More pages of scripture were organized or written during the time our mystery story takes place than during any other 40-year period in history, including the Restoration in the last days.[1] Even Nephi's journey in the Book of Mormon is not larger than this story. In fact, it is an essential *part of it.*

Three of the four Major Prophets[2] of the Old Testament lived during this time. Isaiah, the remaining Major Prophet, prophesied extensively *about* this time. The books of Kings and Chronicles each end their histories with this tale. All roads in the Old Testament lead to a single, massive, climactic epic:

The destruction of Jerusalem in 587 BC the final and complete fall of the Israelite nation from the grace of God.

Did you know?

Up to 1/3 of the Old Testament and Book of Mormon was written by authors who experienced the same historical events.

_{Of the 834,000 words in these books, 214,000 of those words are estimated to have been written by authors that lived in Jerusalem immediately prior to its destruction. This estimate *does not* take into account the books of Kings and Chronicles which would add an additional 80,000 words if they were written during this time period, which appears to be the case. This estimate *does* include the 116 lost pages of the Book of Mormon, the contents of which are unknown. We assume that most of these pages were written by Lehi himself. The word count of these pages is estimated based on surviving hand-written pages of the Book of Mormon manuscripts.}

The Heart of the Hebrew Bible

The destruction of Jerusalem appears to be at the heart of why the Old Testament *even exists*. The Old Testament, with its histories, laws, poetry, music, writings, and prophecies, appears to have been compiled because the Hebrew civilization was disintegrating. The true prophets of the day knew that their heritage and religion would be destroyed. It was only a matter of time. Their goal was to preserve their story in as great of detail as possible so that future generations would not only know the truth of what happened, but also be able to learn from their mistakes. Indeed, it may be said that the Old Testament is a book that attempts to compile all one would need to restore fallen Israel's religion, culture, language, and art.

---

1 Keep in mind the Book of Mormon was not written in the last days, but in ancient times. It was *translated* in the last days.
2 The Major Prophets are Isaiah, Jeremiah, Ezekiel, and Daniel.

The story of the destruction of Jerusalem permeates the writings, prophecies, and purposes of the Old Testament from the Fall of Adam down to the Fall of the Israelite people as recorded in the Book of Jeremiah. It is, in essence, *the* story of the Old Testament. All other stories, along with being tremendous books unto themselves, appear to be organized to provide background for, and context to, the story that was imminent at the doors: the destruction of the Hebrew culture and its true religion.

The Sticks of Judah and Joseph

A prophecy in Ezekiel was fulfilled when, in 1982, the Bible (the Stick of Judah) and the Book of Mormon (the Stick of Joseph) were combined into a single book.[3] However, as Latter-day Saints, when was the last time we read them, talked about them, or thought about them as a single, continuous book?

Scriptures our chronological are not. Sounds a little weird, right? That sentence is difficult to understand because it is out of order. It should read, "Our scriptures are not chronological." When sentences, or books of scripture, are not chronological they become more difficult to understand!

Time and distance have separated the Old Testament from the Book of Mormon in both our Standard Works and in our thoughts. But the facts are: Lehi was contemporary with Jeremiah, Daniel, Ezekiel, Habakkuk, and others in the Old Testament. Lehi's story isn't a *separate* story in a *separate* book, *separated* by 1200 pages of New Testament, Topical Guide, and Bible Dictionary. His story is a *continuation of the story of the Old Testament: the destruction of Jerusalem.* The Book of Mormon contains the final, exciting chapters of that story. Conversely, the Book of Mormon doesn't *begin* with First Nephi. It *began* in the Book of Jeremiah, when Lehi and Nephi were born and where they learned true doctrine and received priesthood power. If we had the first 116 pages of the Book of Mormon (the Lost Book of Lehi)[4] these facts would probably be more self-evident. As it is they must largely be inferred.

Lehi and Nephi were simply continuing their righteous Hebrew heritage of powerful personal revelation accurately recorded on enduring materials. So powerful were their revelations and so enduring was their record that God would choose it to provide the foundation for the dispensation of the fullness of times. This is the time in which we now live.

A Story of Hope, Not Despair

The destruction of Jerusalem is a dark story, a sad story, with a horribly tragic ending. Who wants to tell or even listen to such a tale? It is an unsung ballad because the wrath of God is poured out in full measure on His children. The record of this is there, in the Old Testament, in surprising detail. We don't read it because

---

3 See Ezekiel 37:15-19.

4 See D&C 3.

Jerusalem will become heaps and a den of dragons. See Jeremiah 9:11

it's unbearable. There's simply no hope in the days of Jeremiah. At least, that's the picture that the Old Testament alone paints for its readers.

But for Latter-day Saints, who view the Old Testament through the lens of the Book of Mormon, Jeremiah's time was one of the most hope-filled times in all of history. There was melancholy, no doubt, but there was also tremendous hope for the future. Why else would they have exerted such efforts to compile and preserve the Old Testament? Why else would this time have produced such powerful revelators as Ezekiel, Daniel, Lehi, Nephi, and of course Jeremiah himself? *This is the time of the Hebrew people's darkest trials, but also the time of their greatest triumphs.*

Perhaps their greatest triumph of all was the miraculous preservation of the story of their own destruction.

The Untold Story

And yet this incredible, hope-filled story is not read or told very often. We can highlight "Did You Know" boxes all day long…but just think about it. The historical event that is the instigator for the compilation or writing of *two-thirds* of our modern scriptures[5]…is also virtually undiscussed?[6] Does that make any sense at all? And yet it is true.

---

5   The Old Testament and the Book of Mormon are the two longest books of scripture. Together they constitute 2/3 of the LDS Standard Works. Without the destruction of Jerusalem in 587 BC it is unlikely these books would exist in their present state.

6   This fact rings very true in the Christian world at large, not only in Latter-day Saint circles.

Did you know?

Jeremiah's book is the longest book in the Bible. The next longest is Ezekiel's, a contemporary prophet to Jeremiah.

_{This excludes the Psalms, which was not written by a single author. It's only a few words longer than Jeremiah, anyway.}

Let's try a simple experiment to see for ourselves. Ask yourself the following questions: Do *you personally* know any details about the destruction of Jerusalem? Do you have *any clue* what happens in the Book of Jeremiah? Can you name *even one* story about the prophet Jeremiah?

Nephi built a boat. David slew Goliath. Moses parted the Red Sea. Jeremiah…let's see here…He…uh…wasn't he a bullfrog?[7]

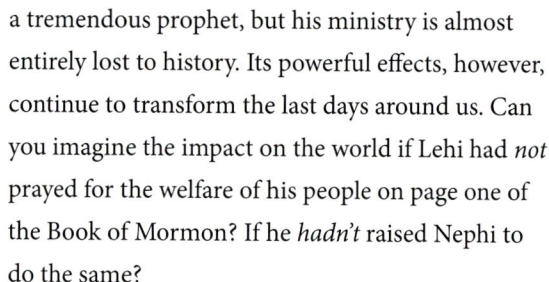

You may be surprised to learn that he was not, in fact, a bullfrog.[8] Jeremiah was a doomsday prophet that spent his entire life trying to save his fallen people. Jeremiah was in Jerusalem *before* it was destroyed. He was in Jerusalem *when* it was destroyed. He was in Jerusalem *after* it was destroyed. He was integral in the compilation and writing of much (if not virtually all) of the Old Testament. He is, quite frankly, one of this world's greatest heroes. His story is entrancing. He and a handful of his followers were responsible for the origination of our scriptures as we know them. We owe them our loyalty and our attention. Among Jeremiah's followers was someone every Latter-day Saint will recognize: the prophet Lehi.

The Lost Book of Lehi

It was Lehi's call to do the *same thing* in the *same place* at the *same time* as Jeremiah. Lehi became a tremendous prophet, but his ministry is almost entirely lost to history. Its powerful effects, however, continue to transform the last days around us. Can you imagine the impact on the world if Lehi had *not* prayed for the welfare of his people on page one of the Book of Mormon? If he *hadn't* raised Nephi to do the same?

Can we, as the benefactors of Lehi's many sacrifices, truly know what it was like for him as a doomsday prophet if we haven't read the Book of Jeremiah, who had the same calling? If we wish to better understand Lehi and his motives, as well as his sons' motives, we should come to a better understanding of the world they lived in and the people they lived with.

You might be asking yourself: is it being suggested that we, as a Latter-day Saint people, may not know Lehi like we *think* we know him?

Yes, my dear reader, that is exactly what I am suggesting.

_{7 "Joy to the World" is a song written by Hoyt Axton, and made famous by the band Three Dog Night in 1971. It opens with the line "Jeremiah was a bullfrog, he was a good friend of mine."}

_{8 In *From the Dust* Jeremiah is inspired by a European Green Toad which lives in Israel. He's not a bullfrog…he's a toad. Surprise!}

Let's consider the stereotypical Lehi. He is an old man in a long white robe with a red shawl on his head. He has a wooden staff which he needs for walking. Like most images of prophets, he is often studying scripture or writing on scrolls. Take a moment. Can you think of any other depiction of Father Lehi than this one?[9]

So…you're telling me that the man that obtained a fortune amidst a nation of thieves, liars, and murderers (but wasn't one himself), that prophesied so powerfully his enemies sought to kill him only shortly after he began his ministry, that helped magnify revelations so pure there are "not many greater,"[10] that successfully led his family across one of the most dangerous deserts in the world (a family that also established two mighty civilizations)…was a frail old man that needed a staff to lean on? I'm not the smartest guy in the world…but…really?

Sariah had two sons in the wilderness. Let me guess…she was 70?

If, in the almost two hundred years we've been reading the Book of Mormon, we haven't painted Lehi's portrait right…are we *sure* we've painted his family right? Are we *sure* we know our Book of Mormon stories like we *think* we know them? If we are not familiar with Jeremiah and the destruction of Jerusalem…can we truly be familiar with Lehi or his son Nephi?

Their time was one of the most dangerous, exciting, and hope-filled times in all of scripture. Their world, their stories, their *lives*, were the root source of the creation of the Old Testament as well as the Book of Mormon. If a fictional exploration into their personalities is valuable, it would be because it may help us come to know them in a way that a doctrinal analysis of their writings cannot. These men literally gave their lives to bring our scriptures to us. Should we not consider putting forth similar effort to bring that story to life?

It is a story that is without a doubt one of the greatest true-life epics ever recorded, if not *the* greatest. We should not only *consider* putting forth that effort, we should maintain it as a *privileged duty*.

---

9   By making this observation I am not discrediting Arnold Frieberg, who we have to thank for this image of Lehi. Quite to the contrary, Frieberg has always been a hero and inspiration of mine and his contributions to Latter-day Saint art are unparalleled.

10   See 2 Nephi 4:2.

Millennia in the Making

After two and a half thousand years, their epic tales will finally be visualized in a powerful storytelling medium. Jeremiah's untold story will be revealed. Ancient Jerusalem will be reborn. The many mysteries that enshroud her tragic fall will be brought to light. Lehi's story, Ezekiel's story, Daniel's story, and Isaiah's story, all of which are connected, will be shared as if you were experiencing it with them. The books of Kings and Chronicles will be laid forth clearly and naturally, like the passing of legends from father to son. The Psalms will be sung by the righteous and the Great Proverbs will guide the pure in heart.

From the Dust

Welcome, dear reader, to the marvelous world of *From the Dust*! As you journey this world alongside the prophets of old you will obtain a clear and powerful understanding of their relationships to each other, to the world they lived in, and to you.

Rather than amplifying the imposing gap of time, culture, and language that separates us from the Old Testament, modern travelers will be able to experience these ancient stories in a way that resonants with them, that "speaks their language." The riches, beauties, and dangers of the Holy Land will be made accessible to newborns and grandparents, to toddlers and teens. Stories seldom shared will experience renewed vigor, longevity, and clarity.

Instead of being a *replacement* to the Holy Scriptures, this carefully designed entertainment is a *supplement* that promotes *interest* and *intrigue* in the scriptures. Readers will be inspired to seek answers to questions and to learn even "by study and also by faith."[11] They will acquire the understanding needed to tackle archaic language. They will obtain a clear understanding of the complex historical and cultural relationships that influenced the creation of the scriptures.

Where Two Worlds Collide

From the Dust is where the ancient and modern worlds meet. Ancient scripture blends with modern art and technology to deliver a creative interpretation that not only entertains, but educates and edifies concerning the beautiful, awe-inspiring, yet sorrowful tale of the fall of a chosen people. Two and a half millennia this tale has waited. Finally, the story of the Hebrew people, as recorded in the Old Testament and the Book of Mormon, is coming to life!

Hopefully, it will prove worth the wait!

---

11 See D&C 88:118.

DID YOU KNOW?

From the Dust was born on February 6, 2011 from doodles drawn during a Bible study class.

Lehi leads his family into the wilderness. See 1 Nephi 2.

The Series

Seasons and Chapters
of From the Dust

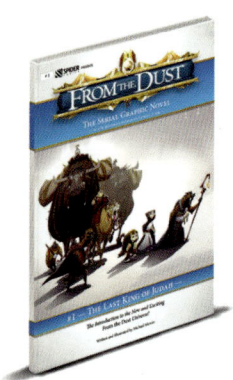  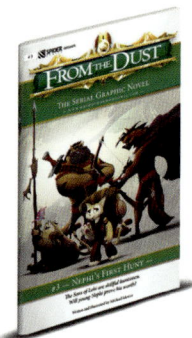 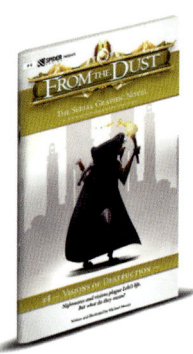

> *The Christian may now perceive that all his bents and faculties have a purpose...he may now, perhaps, fairly dare to guess that in Fantasy he may actually assist [God] in the effoliation and multiple enrichment of creation.*
>
> — J.R.R. Tolkien

Every page of *From the Dust* is a celebration of art, music, poetry, and imagination. These universal languages speak to the human soul. We promise your heart will strengthen, your life will enrich, and your understanding will increase concerning the beautiful Hebraic heritage that *billions* of us share in common — Jew, Christian, and Muslim alike.[1]

The *From the Dust* series takes you on an epic journey that starts in Jerusalem's darkest hour and leads readers progressively through the journeys of prophets that lived at the time of Jerusalem's destruction. The series will last for years with new chapters released regularly. Each issue consists of a complete story, or "chapter," consisting of 24-36 pages of full-color story. In addition, each issue contains supplementary educational material.

The *From the Dust* series is also divided into seasons. *From the Dust #1: The Last King of Judah* marks the start of *Season 1: Departure*. In *Season 1* we become familiar with the fallen world that our heroes live in. It is a world wild with depravity, a world of darkness and deceit — where no one can be trusted except a few devout followers of Yahweh.

---

[1] These three religions are called Abrahamic religions. Each believes that the Hebrew Bible is sacred and each traces its heritage back to Abraham. We have far more in common than we have different!

Doctrine

From the Dust isn't Sunday School, but it *is* educational. It does not define doctrine (like Sunday School does) but rather provides additional insights on non-doctrinal subjects which may prove helpful in understanding the stories and characters of the scriptures.

This allows *From the Dust* to become a tool in the hands of students and educators. Readers can intimately and vicariously experience dramatic events, both real and fantasized, without having to be put in spiritual or physical danger.

Relational Accuracy

From the Dust is a work of *fiction* primarily designed to entertain audiences. In addition, *From the Dust* is designed to establish in the minds of readers clear *relational accuracy*. This can sometimes come at the expense of scriptural details. Here's an example:

In 1 Ne. 2:16, Nephi says he was both "exceedingly young" and "large in stature." Most visual interpretations to date clearly portray Nephi's being "large in stature." However, such an interpretation has often come at the expense of Nephi's prior declaration that he was "exceedingly young." Which of these scriptural details is most important when trying to understand who Nephi was? The answer: neither.

No matter how old or large Nephi was, the important *relationship* is that Nephi was the *youngest of four brothers, none of whom were married*. When communicating scriptural *relationships* accurately is our priority (rather than focusing on getting all the details perfect), suddenly Lehi's family becomes a surprisingly normal family of teenage boys. Could it have been so? Read your scriptures again and decide for yourself!

Be aware that many non-scriptural personalities are integral for the *From the Dust* storyline to function; in particular, many women of the scriptures who are rarely mentioned will play clear and powerful roles in *From the Dust* — for both good and evil.

Violence, Drugs, and Immorality

The ancient world was a dangerous place for both the body and the spirit. While *From the Dust* visualizes these dangers, it never glorifies violence or immoral behavior of any kind. If *From the Dust* were a movie, it would have a strong PG rating. Parental guidance is suggested.

An Entertainment Tool

From the Dust does not downplay the existence of evil. Rather, it confronts evil in ways conducive to a family environment. *From the Dust* asks moral questions of its readers but rarely answers those questions. This allows readers — and the parents of readers — the opportunity to answer these real-life questions themselves. Parents will find *From the Dust* has the teaching versatility sorely needed, but rarely available, in spiritual entertainment.

From the Dust is a unique and effective tool that brings scriptural ideas, characters, stories, and facts to the family's daily conversations. We hope you enjoy reading *From the Dust* as much as we enjoy making it!

From the Dust will assuredly help anyone to build a foundation of faith grounded in scriptural knowledge and experience.

HEBREW

.HSI-WERBEH YLNO ,HSILGNE EKIL TSUJ S'TI

WELL...MAYBE NOT JUST LIKE IT.

Hebrew is the original language of the **Old Testament**. It is read **right to left**. Learning Hebrew not only enriches your **understanding of the scriptures**, but also your understanding of the **people** who **wrote them**.

From the Dust's Hebrew Learning Edition **progressively teaches you** the Hebrew alphabet and to read **backwards**. (Well, forwards in Hebrew...) The Hebrew Learning Edition **comes as part** of each *From the Dust* Multi-Touch Book.

WWW.**BOOKOFMORMONCOMIC**.COM

COMING SOON.

Only for iPad.

Above: Portion of the Temple Scroll, labeled 11Q19, one of the longest of the Dead Sea Scrolls.

THE CAST

TRUE LEGENDS

of From the Dust

> "*If you would not be forgotten as soon as you are dead, either write something worth reading or do things worth writing.*"
>
> — Benjamin Franklin

Modern prophets have declared that the disintegration of the family will bring upon the world the worst calamities foretold in the Bible. The details of these horrific prophecies will be omitted for the time being, but before the storyline of *From the Dust* is over we will visit many of them.

Fortunately, by prophesying the root cause of the Bible's worst calamities, our prophets have also given us the solution to them: save the family, save the world.

It is family relationships, individually developed by each of us, that will ultimately provide the strength and power we will need to accomplish the monumental tasks ahead of us. It was so anciently, it will be so today. Never were they easy, ever were they worth it.

Families can not only be *together forever*, but *together* they can *change the world forever*.

And that's exactly what this incredible family *did*.

Lehi prays for the welfare of his people. See 1 Nephi 1:5.

Lehi

A business maven who's genius and integrity have earned him respect throughout the known world.

Lehi was a poor child who led a rough, desert life. But he was born with a gift: he's a visionary. He can't help himself. While a youth his big dreams held little clout, but after mastering the craft of metalworking, they have made him exorbitantly wealthy. No longer a craftsman, he now runs a highly successful international trade network. His reputation precedes him wherever he goes.

Unfortunately, Lehi's career skills are of little use in the small-time environment of his family, where he struggles like any father to teach his children correct principles. He is often unconsciously hard on his sons, especially his birthright son, Laman, who is the principle heir of his fortunes. Lehi sees too much of his own violent desert heritage in Laman — and it reminds him of a past he desperately wants to forget.

When a majestic vision turns his life upside down, Lehi finds himself at the forefront of a dangerous religio-political resistance that will try his courage, faith, and strength to their uttermost limits and beyond.

Sariah

A smart, educated woman of high class but pragmatic character.

Sariah is a woman with a singular spirit. From the time of her youth she has had a strong will of her own, but ever has she sought the welfare of others. She loves to build community environments: in her family, in her home town, in her nation — everywhere. For Sariah, life is meaningless without people to fill it up.

Twenty years ago she fell in love with Lehi for his bravado and courage and she has never fallen out of love since. Her family is her joy. Whereas Lehi struggles as a father, Sariah is a born nurturer. She knows what her children need, and she does her best to give it to them, be it discipline, care, attention, or

Sariah enjoys the land of her inheritance.

freedom. Her worst fear is to see her children give in to their more carnal natures...or succumb to the physical and spiritual dangers of her fallen nation.

Her family life has required from her enormous energy. Laman, her eldest, has been more than a handful to raise. Temperamental and strong, he has tested Sariah's patience since his birth. His brother Lemuel only magnified the trouble. Sariah has discovered her children are far more talented and intelligent than she will ever be. As such, she has learned to rely heavily on the whisperings of the Spirit. More often than not her family's unique struggles have left her with nowhere else to turn but Yahweh Himself.

Sariah's Hebrew heritage can be traced back to Abraham, and from Father Abraham all the way back to Adam. A part of her family has always been faithful and she is determined to continue that noble tradition.

Sariah comforts Laman after his first temper tantrum.

Laman

A talented, athletic young man who does everything right — at least, so it appears on the outside.

Laman, although still a teenager, is already known and respected in many places as the Heir of Lehi. As Lehi's eldest son, Laman bears the birthright. Lehi has trained, educated, and prepared him in every way possible for his ultimate inheritance of the family business, its fortunes, and its reputation.

Laman's life has been one of rigorous expectations. His father's standards are high — so high, in fact, that Laman has struggled to meet them, despite his powerful strength and keen intelligence. On the one hand, Lehi's standards have helped push Laman to be the top in his class — both athletically and academically — but on the other, they have filled Laman's life with stress. Sometimes, when the circumstances have been difficult, Laman has chosen to utilize less-than-honest means to achieve his goals. It has allowed him more time to do the things he loves — hunting, traveling, and spending time with his friends — while at the same time keeping his father off his back. Although he knows his father would disapprove, Laman is reaching a point where he wonders if anything could truly placate his father's seemingly insatiable — and unattainable — dreams.

At the end of the day, Laman knows he's set for life — the family fortune is enormous, the family business is strong, and his birthright inheritance is guaranteed…provided he doesn't break the rules *too* much.

Laman hunts a wild beast in Arabia. See 1 Nephi 16:14.

Lemuel

A muscly male with little tact and no agenda.

Lemuel is largely a product of his environment. If it weren't for his elder brother Laman he wouldn't really know what to do with himself. They are two halves of the same trouble-making spirit — Laman the cunning mastermind and Lemuel the willing, durable participant. They've been known to pick a few fights — but not lose them.

Don't let Lemuel's refined and educated upbringing fool you. The last thing on his mind is high culture. When he cooks, it's in a blender. When he womanizes, it's with a club. If he were able to schedule his own time rather than follow his father's rigorous routines he'd…he'd…wait a second…what's a "schedule" again?

I'm going fishing.

SAM

Nice guy, but gun-shy.

There isn't anything that Sam can't fear. Life is nervous. Sam's only solace is pleasing people, but try *that* in *this* family. Poor Sam's efforts to mediate peace are dismissed before they begin. He is the forgotten middle child, neglected and ignored. If he could find where he put his place in life he would gladly sit on it forevermore.

Unlike his elder brothers who are intelligent, strong, and confident, Sam struggles just to get by. He's not good at all that "guy" stuff — like hunting, or picking fights. In fact, Sam's not really good at…well, at most things, really.

Sam's only significant bond in the family is with his mother — in the kitchen. It's the one place he finds himself able to be useful. In a family of extraordinary talent and brilliant minds the kitchen brings peace and a chance for him to participate — at least, until the dinner table is set and the conversations begin.

Although Sam is nothing like his family, time will show that he's a vital and important member of it — that extra ingredient that really makes the meal complete. Its presence is so subtle you don't really notice it… until you've run out.

Nephi does his best to do his part. As the youngest it's often his job to do menial tasks — washing the dishes, carrying the supplies, or running errands. But his father taught him that even the smallest tasks, when executed well and with diligence, make a powerful, meaningful difference. And Nephi believes his father.

Nephi has spent most of his lifetime in the land of his family's inheritance. The entire family has been involved with the construction of Lehi's Estate, a fine manor located in a mountain valley near Hebron. The beautiful home was designed by Lehi and continues to be refined by Sariah and the rest of the family. Nephi helps his mother daily as they terrace the hillside, build gardens and walls, and prepare the estate for lifelong residency.

Circumstance will reveal that little Nephi is mighty strong. The fate of his family — and his people — will one day rest on his small shoulders.

NEPHI

A stalwart youth who abhors violence and loves the simple life.

Nephi is a multi-talented prodigy...but a 12-year-old one. No one knows that his destiny is to become a legend...least of all him.

As the youngest of four brothers Nephi has to work extra hard to keep up — and the amazing thing is — *he does*. His remarkable accomplishments are often overlooked because of their simplicity, but it does not change their significance. When his hard work does get overlooked, he makes it a point not to let it get him down.

Jeremiah blesses Nephi as a kitten.

Jeremiah

An unconventional but highly charismatic prophet who never gives up. Ever.

Quirky, small, and funny-looking, Jeremiah has never been popular with the ruling class, despite the fact that he has been an advisor to multiple kings. While still a tadpole, Yahweh called him as a prophet. The weight of his assignment — to cry repentance during Jerusalem's darkest hour — has forced him to cling to all things lively and fun just to guard from eternal depression. He is not only *a* prophet, but *the* prophet, and the remnant of loyal followers of Yahweh follow his divinely inspired lead. His patience and long-suffering are truly inspiring.

Jeremiah's father, Hilkiah the Priest, discovered lost scripture in the Holy Temple while Jeremiah was still a boy.[1] Known in the last days as the Book of Deuteronomy,[2] these scriptures contained the prophecies concerning the destruction of Jerusalem and the horrors that should befall the Holy City should the Covenant People fall from grace.

Now, knowing the destruction of his people is imminent, Jeremiah and the loyal followers of Yahweh dedicate themselves to collecting and preserving the remnants of their dying culture.

---

1 See 2 Kings 22:8-14 and Jeremiah 1:1. While it is possible the Hilkiah in these verses is two separate individuals, *From the Dust* assumes that they are not.

2 Many scholars suggest that the "lost book" spoken of contained parts of the Book of Deuteronomy, specifcally its final chapters. This is because of King Josiah's reaction to the book. What exactly the "lost book" contained remains a mystery. *From the Dust* assumes that the lost book was indeed the suggested parts of Deuteronomy.

Nebuchadrezzar

The austere Lord of the Chaldeans, the King of Babylon.

Lord Nebuchadrezzar is fierce and ruthless in the establishment of his new empire. He drives conquered peoples into submission by banishing the ruling class to be assimilated permanently into Babylonian culture. He does not tolerate disobedience. He is determined to rule the world — and he will, for a short time. Even the 2000-year-old Egyptian dynasties will fall to him.

In addition, Lord Drezzar (as he is often called since his full name is unpronounceable) is destined to destroy Jerusalem and its people into dust. He will take the treasures of his military campaigns (including treasures from the Holy Temple) and build the Hanging Gardens — one of the seven Great Wonders of the Ancient World.

Lord Drezzar watches the Holy Temple of Yahweh burn to ashes.

Pashur

An educated, evil elitist that will work any situation to his advantage with lies, treachery, deceit, and violence.

Pashur is the Chief Priest of the Temple, and the Prophet of the Church of Yahweh. His entire life he has slowly, subtly, and craftily increased his power. Now he rules Jerusalem in every way except by holding the royal scepter. His obsession to be king drives all his actions. The only way to become so is to manipulate and destroy the culture and religion of the Israelites until they will accept someone not of the house of David on the throne. He will go to any lengths to make this happen, including making sacrifices to pagan gods.

Pashur's heart is cold, callused, and cowardly. Despite his wolfish size he will do anything to mitigate physical harm to himself. His lying tongue is his greatest weapon, and Jeremiah the Prophet is his life-long enemy. Indeed, it was Pashur who beat Jeremiah and threw him in the stocks above the Holy Temple of Yahweh...

Zedekiah

The weak puppet-king of Judah. What little power he obtained from his coronation corrupted him instantly.

Zedekiah was a largely forgotten (or ignored) heir to the throne of Judah, that is, until Lord Drezzar needed a new puppet. Zedekiah is the last king in a long stream of thinning blood. The legacy of his forebears have left him little foundation on which to build his rule. The power and majesty that the King of Judah once held is now long departed. Princes, priests, and others vie for control of the city, her wealth, and her holy places. The King is but a pawn in a complex soap opera of deceit, lies, murder, and betrayal. Add to this hellish recipe the naive and selfish demeanor of Zedekiah and it is no wonder his example will lead the Holy City to her doom.

Though he was installed on the throne at age twenty-one, Zedekiah refuses to act like anything but a two-year-old. Spoiled and spiteful, this young man abuses his servants and his people for sport. At least, that's when he has the energy for it. Most of his life has been spent in apathy, and it has only amplified since he was given the royal scepter.

Solomon

Under his great leadership the Tribes of Israel thrived.

Solomon is one of Israel's greatest and most influential kings. The People of Israel flourished under his noble and measured rule. Perhaps most notable of Solomon's virtues was his righteous ability to judge. His wisdom exceeded that of any other, and the fame of it spread so far that royalty from other nations traveled hundreds of miles to entreat his advice. Solomon justly upheld the laws of the kingdom as well as the laws of Moses.

Solomon's father David left him a complex but powerful legacy. David's legendary life cannot be equalled by any subsequent king of Israel; it is rich in its glory and evocative in its humanity. Above any material possession Solomon inherited from his father, it was David's ideals and morals that most influenced his son. David was a unique and dynamic leader who maintained a vision for his country, his people, and his religion far beyond the imagination of previous generations. David willed an empire into existence, but it was his son Solomon who ruled it and beautified it.

Solomon learned from his father a deep love of the arts. A flourishing of songs and poetry testified of a new renaissance of knowledge, wisdom, and inspiration that enlightened the people of Israel. Never was there a happier time among them...but it was not without its darkness. Indeed, both David and Solomon had hidden secrets that would bring about the fall of their short-lived kingdom.

Although not fully realized in their own lifetime, the consequences of the choices of David and Solomon continued to influence for evil the kings of the Israelite nation, even down until Jerusalem's final hour. And thus we see that the destiny of a nation can sometimes be tied to the choice of a single individual on a single night of his life...

THE FIRST FAN KIT

A UNIQUE COLLECTIBLE

- **Hand-signed** and **numbered** by Michael Mercer
- **Contains** *From the Dust* #0, Spider Comics' **first publication**
- A **54-card deck** of playing cards with **From the Dust characters**
- **5 Unique** Bookmarks
- **5 Art Prints** with stories **on the back** (8.5" x 5.5")
- The **"Hope Whispers"** poster (19"x27")

EVERYTHING YOU NEED IN ONE PLACE.

Before *From the Dust* #1, **Spider Comics** published *From the Dust* #0: *Things to Come*. As the title **implies**, *From the Dust* #0 is a **44-page** collectible promotional comic with **tons of unique accessories** including **playing cards**, a poster, artprints, and **bookmarks!**

WWW.BOOKOFMORMONCOMIC.COM

THE WORLD

DANGEROUS EMPIRES
of From the Dust

> *"And it came to pass that Enoch looked upon the earth; and he heard a voice from the bowels thereof, saying: Wo, wo is me, the mother of men; I am pained, I am weary, because of the wickedness of my children. When shall I rest, and be cleansed from the filthiness which is gone forth out of me?"*
>
> — Moses 7:48

Many years have passed since the time of Solomon the Wise. The forces of evil have grown tremendously powerful. The people of Judah are no longer players in the world's affairs, only spectators. Rather than leading as a lion, Judah cowers like an alley cat.

Jeremiah the prophet stands as a brass wall against the tide of destruction that threatens the Kingdom of Judah. He leads an ever-shrinking number of loyal followers of Yahweh. They seek answers to the spiritual heartaches that plague their society, but they struggle to live righteously in their wicked nation. Add to this the power-hungry lusts of the surrounding empires who see lesser, disunited kingdoms like Judah as pawns, and there can be only one inevitable outcome: war.

War was a part of everyone's life, not just the military. Few people could grow to adulthood without experiencing first-hand the effects of bloodshed. It was not distant. It was not virtual. It was human and it was horrible. It was life and death. War killed families. War caused famine. War destroyed happiness.

The world of *From the Dust* is a world of constant warfare. Physical. Spiritual. Personal. And the empires of humanity were the cause of them.

The world of FROM THE DUST

BABYLON

JUDAH

EGYPT

ARABIA

Babylon
The City of Towers.

The Euphrates river divides the city of Babylon.

Anciently, in the days before Father Abraham, Babylon's pride grew so tall it called down divine wrath upon the world. People became cursed, scattered, and tribal. Now, 2000 years later, Babylon's towers are rising to new heights as her evil empire expands once again. Chaldea, Ur, Kish and other sister-states have been conquered by Nabopolassar, a Chaldean Lord. The Great Assyrian Empire has crumbled and the new Babylonia has emerged.

Like its predecessors, this new Empire of Babylon is ruthless and prideful. Hammurabi, an ancient ruler, instilled in his people a Code of Law that brought harsh order. It was simple: an eye for an eye and a tooth for a tooth. If you take life unlawfully, your life will be taken as payment. These laws were as effective as they were bloody. Their impact on society, and the world, continue even to the last days.

Babylonian Culture

Every aspect of Babylonian society is designed to support the cause of the Emperor. Babylon not only conquers a nation with her military might, but also conquers its culture. The ruling class of the conquered nation is relocated to the heart of Babylon. These individuals are given positions of honor and power. They are well-respected. But all this is merely a ploy to destroy the conquered nation's identity, culture, and religion. By making friends of their most powerful enemies, Babylon simultaneously destroys her enemies and strengthens her empire. It is an insidious and powerful weapon of war.

Such privileged treatment, however, was not received by the common man. Only the educated, ruling class was respected. The poor, the weak, and the uneducated were considered useless fodder, good for nothing but to be trodden under foot or cast out. These unfortunate souls were left to fend for themselves, but lacked the skills to do so. Their society often became controlled by criminals free to fill the power vacuum left by the assimilated leaders and craftsmen.

The Great City

Babylon the Great has massive city walls so wide a chariot with four horses can run the top of them. The city is divided by the beautiful Euphrates river running through its midst. Luxurious temples to dragon gods rise from the inner city, and dragons decorate the kingdom everywhere. Fierce lions and wild beasts are honored with statues. The most deadly animals are considered worthy of royalty and are hunted for sport.

Babylon's towers rise higher than any other. They can be seen from every direction throughout the heartland of their empire.

Egypt

The Everlasting Empire.

Egypt's empire is protected by a wealth of food and a natural desert barrier.

As long as the world has stood, so, too, has the Everlasting Empire.

For thousands of years Egypt has been the world's center of culture, art, and military might. Their lush wetlands, replenished yearly by the flooding of the great Iteru River (known in the last days as the Nile) has provided this nation a never-ending supply of grain, which is stored for protection from deadly famine. This bounty has provided the nation unparalleled longevity.

Egypt has led the world technologically and artistically for millennia. The Egyptians were the world's first and most ambitious scribes, artists, scientists, and architects. As pioneers, they had no one but themselves to depend on for means or abilities. They developed sophisticated writing, paper, engineering, irrigation, and much more.

Papyrus, the first paper, was developed in Egypt long ago and became the foundation on which their many accomplishments were created. Like modern paper, they used papyrus for business, for legal documents, for education, and for artwork.

Painting, dying, pottery, and all things artistic were the especial talent of the Egyptians. Their writing, which included the radiant hieroglyphs, powerfully exemplified the Egyptian love of color, shape, beauty, and storytelling. Indeed, Egyptian hieroglyphs could be called the first cartoons and the walls of Egyptian temples the first graphic novels.

In addition, the Egyptians were some of the world's first metallurgists, working copper, iron, gold and even mercury with fine precision. Glass was also an Egyptian invention, used for thousand of years before the time of Lehi.

They developed many sciences including astronomy, chemistry, medicine, and mathematics. They used the knowledge they obtained to improve their craftsmanship and daily life.

The sheer time, size, and wealth the Egyptians had at their disposal produced architectural splendors that, even in the last days, are breathtaking to behold. Over three thousand years of growth, development, and technology empowered Egyptian cities. The grandeur of Egypt in the days of Lehi overshadowed all other empires in glory.

But that grandeur had come at a price. The Egyptians were a slave-keeping society that abused the precious lives of others, and this they did for personal gain. They exacted tribute from neighboring countries, sometimes enslaving entire nations to meet the demands of their empire's monumental building projects.

The Hebrew people have an intimate relationship with Egypt. In the days of Joseph, Abraham's great-grandson, the people of Israel were one of the nations that Egypt enslaved. They spent over 400 years in captivity before Yahweh raised up Moses to deliver them.

The Hebrew people call the land of Egypt "Mizraim" and the Old Testament states that these people are the descendants of Ham, the son of Noah.

Arabia

The Desert of Fortunes.

Arabia is a harsh desert landscape.

Wealth is the crux of this lawless realm of independent tribes and nations. Through this hostile land runs the incense trail, a loosely-defined, dangerous road for wealthy merchants and hearty travelers. The trail leads through the great cities of Arabia that dot the wadis[1] of the desert and provide relative security in a world of danger. Outside of these secluded one-city nations is a vast wasteland where only wild beasts and the Bedu tribes that hunt them can survive. These tribes are far different from the Tribes of Israel, who wandered the desert in relative peace. The ancient Beduin found honor only in piracy. Without plunder they could not exist.

For those powerful enough to protect their caravans, the incense trade became as lucrative as gold mining. Untold wealth flowed into Arabia from India, Africa, Babylon, Egypt, and Canaan. It was a time of tremendous prosperity for the nations of Arabia.

But so arid were these areas that the wealth of these nations was kept to the relative few. Unlike

---

[1] Valleys. Pronounced WAH-dees

Egypt, Babylon, or even Judah, Arabia had no constant source of fertility. Little rain and blazing heat made these regions inhabitable. Compared to the populated metropolises of Egypt and Babylon, Arabia was sparsely settled. Without the resources of people and labor, Arabia never built wonders to match those of Egypt or Babylon.

The only consistency in Arabia was that wealth, somehow or another, would shift hands, be it from violence, trade, or old age. Unlike the great Code of Hammurabi, which was enforced universally on an entire empire, each nation in Arabia has individual kings and queens with unique laws. Indeed, it could be said that each king or queen *was* the law.

Sheba

Arabia is famed in Judah not only for its incense, but also because the Queen of Sheba traveled from this land to visit Solomon the Wise many years ago. She brought tremendous gifts to his kingdom and established a peaceful relationship. Unfortunately, the time of peace between these kingdoms is long passed.

JUDAH
The Home of From the Dust.

Judah is a mountain country with thousands of years of history.

The Kingdom of Judah is all that is left of the once great Empire of Israel. Three hundred years before Lehi, King David united the Twelve Tribes of Israel and established a great empire. During that time, the Israelite culture experienced its greatest flourishing of arts and sciences. Engineers created great monuments and artisans beautified them beyond compare. Nations came from afar to see the glory of Israel and to pay tribute to her kings. All the land from Euphrates in the north to the Red Sea in the south was Israel.

David's son, Solomon the Wise, built the great Temple of Yahweh, a symbol of the spiritual blessings bestowed upon the people of Israel. In the temple they made great covenants with Him, including the covenant to obey the laws of the great prophet Moses, who led their people miraculously out of Egypt and through the desert. The House of Israel gave their noblest efforts to the Temple's construction, sacrificing great worldly treasures to create an everlasting testament of their dedication to Yahweh. The Temple represents the best of their beauty, strength, perseverance, and endurance.

But those ideals and that glory have long since faded. Now the Empire of Israel is little more than a city-state. The Holy Temple is majestic as it ever was, but during these dark days its sanctity has become polluted, desecrated and abused. Indeed, even those most worthy to walk its corridors have been cast out — including the prophet Jeremiah himself. The history of the Fall of the House of Israel shall yet be told in full. It is a long tale, and worth the telling.

Judah, a Hill Country

The kingdom of Judah is a hill country with so little flat land that farmers must terrace the hillsides for their gardens. Shepherds and their sheep are plentiful. They build their cities on the tops of the mountains for defense and ease of communication within their nation. Judah's mountain roads are little more than paths; there is little protection on them. As you travel Judah you will see the remnants of the many shortcomings of the people of Israel. Ruins are everywhere.

Jerusalem, Judah's capital, is a divided city, with one foot in verdant paradise and the other in the Valley of Death, where the Salt Sea lies.

Hebron

Hebron, the soul of Judah, the City of Patriarchs, the place where Abraham, Isaac, and Jacob are buried. Abraham himself chose this spot as a resting place for his noble family. It has been sacred to the people of Israel ever since.

David became King of Judah in Hebron, and later Lord of the Empire of Israel. Only after establishing his right to rule in Hebron did David move the government of his empire to Jerusalem, which became known as the City of David.

The Hebron region lies a day's journey due south of Jerusalem and consists of hill country rich for agriculture, but come summer they are blown dry with the hot, East Arabian winds.

Pagan Altars

The less faithful of Judah, contrary to divine commands, often worshipped "other gods" and built altars to these deities in a variety of locations. These removed sites witnessed human atrocities so appalling only the Bible can tell them.

Lachish

Lachish was the next most important Judahite city besides Jerusalem, the capital. Rich in pasture and rich in rain, the Lachish region blooms in spring with lush carpets of flowers. Grass-covered limestone formations emerge from the landscape like watchful guardians.

Lachish itself was once a great fortress, a giant stronghold that stood as a barrier between Philistine and Israel. The open landscape provided advanced warning of approaching armies and the mighty fortress walls, built in many layers, proved an impossible barrier for all but the mightiest of armies. The armies of Sennecherib, however, proved their might during the days of Isaiah, and Lachish fell. That was over a hundred years ago.

Although the fortress has been rebuilt, it will never again know its former glory. Even the bounty of

The Valley of Death

Less than a day's journey southeast of Jerusalem is the Valley of Death, where the sister-cities of Sodom and Gomorrah once stood. All that is left of these nations is salt and ash. Yahweh burned their wickedness from before His face. The ruins of Sodom and Gomorrah remain a vivid reminder of the vile depths to which human behavior can sink. Travelers through this black land will see the scars of heavenly fire that still fester the earth.

the earth's harvest in this region has now become tainted by the impure actions of its inhabitants. Lachish, like all of Judah, is but a shadow of her former self, sustained only by the sacrifices of her predecessors.

Many traders passed through this area of Judah, and many travelers headed north or south would have no reason to deviate course and go up to Jerusalem in the mountains. For them, Lachish is all that they know of the mysterious and seclusive mountain people of Judah.

The Negev

On the southern border of Hebron and Lachish lay the Negev, the Great Desert of Israel. This dry landscape harbors only a few shepherds who must constantly travel to keep their flocks fed. Father Abraham and his family constructed wells in Beersheba, a city on the edge of the Negev. It was here that his son Isaac built an altar, and Isaac's son Jacob had a dream about a stairway to heaven.

Beersheba is the southernmost settlement of Judah, although many, many miles of the inhabitable Negev continue southward.

DID YOU KNOW?

Abraham's grandson Jacob was renamed Israel. The "People of Israel" means "the People of Jacob."

Jerusalem
The Mountain Citadel of Judah.

Jerusalem was once a place of beauty and splendor.

It is said that in the days of Abraham a great prince took upon himself the covenants of the high priesthood. Many had come before, and many after, but none were greater. His legend would last millennia. He cried repentance unto his people with power, leading them from being ruled by wickedness to being ruled by peace and love. He was Melchizedek, the Prince of Peace, the great King of Salem.

Jeru*salem* is thought to be the land of Salem where Melchizedek once ruled. Rich in righteous heritage, this land is a precious gift, a realm of security, a sanctuary for revelation, law, and priesthood. It is a land of stark destiny. From the time of Abraham it became divided by the Covenant — not physically, no, but spiritually a rift occurred the instant the Covenant was made. To those who entered it an eternal bond was formed leading them inevitably closer to Yahweh if they obeyed. But those not under the Covenant lacked the spiritual blessings and guidance of such a bond.

The Covenant was entered by the entire House of Israel and it made them a nation of priests — a special people, separate and secluded, but with promises so great they enveloped the world. These promises, however, would not be realized without tremendous hardships. The House of Israel became the world's pioneers in priestly living, an example since her infancy of how to live under Covenant — and how not to.

Jerusalem and the mountains of Ephraim in which it sits has ever been the home of kingliness and priesthood, but also iniquity and priestcraft. That kingliness is born of priesthood principles, but that iniquity…comes from the darker corners of the earth.

Jerusalem now holds the leaders of all that is left of the dying House of Israel. Some families lead because they have inherited wealth. These are the princes. Others lead because they have inherited priesthood. These are the priests. Still others lead because they have inherited royal blood. These are the kings. Few, if any, lead as Melchizedek once did: by taking upon themselves the covenants of the high priesthood and wielding its power for righteousness. The power of the priesthood, despite the prophets' greatest efforts, is dying.

Many of Jerusalem's inhabitants have only been in Jerusalem a few generations. It is no longer a city of the Tribe of Judah, but a home for all the remnant of Israel. They fled to its protective care during the Great Destruction in the days of Isaiah 100 years ago. It was here, in Jerusalem, that the last stand of the people of Israel was held. But Yahweh granted us one last chance to repent of our evil…a chance that is almost dried up…

The Story

Season 1: Departure

For Jeremiah, the great prophet.

*One day we want to hear how it all **really** went down. Until then, however, here's our best effort at getting it right.*

Thank you so much...for everything!

Chapter 1

The Last King of Judah

For a thousand years my people, the House of Israel, have struggled against the powers of darkness. Ancient prophecies foretell the time when our iniquities will make us ripe for destruction...a time that is no longer distant, but nigh. Jerusalem will fall and the Holy Temple, the House of Yahweh himself, will be burned into ashes...into dust.

In these, the dying years of my civilization, there are but few that remain true. The promises of the fathers, however, shall never be forgotten. If we prove faithful we will be led to a land of freedom: a place where the Laws of Moses can be upheld properly in faith, purity, and righteousness.

But in this wicked hour it is difficult to believe that such a land could exist. The light of our nation has dwindled quickly. Even our kings are little more than puppets in the hands of the Evil One...

OUR HEARTS WERE PURE. THERE WAS NO EVIL THAT COULD DIVIDE US.

WE HAD WON THE LAND OF OUR FATHERS, AT LONG LAST.

THE PROMISED LAND.

...DAD?

THAT DESTRUCTION SHALL COME UPON ALL WORKERS OF DARKNESS, WHEN THEY ARE FULLY RIPE.

:SOB:

UHHH...

AND I DESIRE THAT THIS, MY PEOPLE, MIGHT NOT BE DESTROYED.

BUT IT IS TOO LATE.

AS QUICKLY AS THE HOUSE OF ISRAEL ROSE, IT FELL.

DID YOU SEE THE LOOK ON HIS FACE? HE NEVER SUSPECTED US!

HA! HA! HA! IT'S BUSINESS TIME!

LOOKY! LOOKY! I GOT A **DONKEY!**

..YES...I NOTICED...

NOW, 300 YEARS LATER, MY PEOPLE ARE A LOST AND FALLEN EMPIRE, DROWNING IN THEIR OWN INIQUITY.

THERE IS NO HOPE LEFT FOR US. WE HAVE BROKEN THE PROMISE OF THE LAND. **YAHWEH, THE GREAT LAWGIVER,** MUST FULFILL THE COVENANT HE MADE WITH US...

FOR WE WERE TO FULFILL THE PROMISE OF THE LAND...OR ELSE ENDURE ITS CURSE –

MEANWHILE, IN THE KING'S PALACE...

...A PARTY WAS GOING ON.

NICE PARTY.

YEAH.

BETTER THAN LAST NIGHT'S FOR SURE.

HONEY ARE YOU SURE ABOUT THIS? DON'T YOU REMEMBER WHAT HAPPENED THE LAST TIME?

ZZZ...

THAT ITH SO COOL!

≶HIC≶

AHA!

ANOTHER ONE!

— AND THEN SHE WAS LIKE —

≶YAWN≶

— AND I WAS LIKE — ≶GASP≶

ABNER! WHAT'S THAT!

THERE... THROUGH THAT WINDOW... IS THAT A —

HE WON'T BE WALKING OUT OF HERE WITH MUCH....

Scriptures

Writings of Prophets
The Most Precious Books on Earth.

> *"And what thank they the Jews for the Bible which they receive from them? Yea, what do the Gentiles mean? Do they remember the travails, and the labors, and the pains of the Jews, and their diligence unto me, in bringing forth salvation unto the Gentiles?"*
>
> — 2 Nephi 29:4-5

The scriptures are overflowing with poetry, imagery, and insights. In many cases, especially with the Old Testament, the scriptures themselves were carefully crafted works of art designed by prophets for specific reasons. Symbolism, allegory, and other forms of figurative language permeate the scriptures. To truly understand the language of our ancient forebears, we need to study their world, their lives, and their culture. All of these subjects combine to provide inspiration for the visuals and storyline of *From the Dust*. The following pages reveal the enormous amount of scriptures that pertain to this first chapter. So much occurs in our opening chapters it may take some time to get through it, but fear not — the scriptures aren't — and never have been — boring! When properly understood, they are the most fascinating and faith-promoting documents that exist. They are records of some of the most intense real-life drama this world has ever seen! Educational sections like this one separate the *facts* from the *fiction*.

Genesis 14:18, KJV

And Melchizedek king of Salem brought forth bread and wine: and he was the priest of the most high God.

1000 years before David, Melchizedek ruled this same land, and built a civilization of peace and prosperity. Since that time, the people had fallen…but that is a story for another day.

Keep a lookout for this Melchizedek fellow. He is barely mentioned in scripture but is one of its most successful leaders!

1 Kings 2:1-4, KJV

Now the days of David drew nigh that he should die; and he charged Solomon his son, saying, I go the way of all the earth: be thou strong therefore, and shew thyself a man;

And keep the charge of the Lord thy God, to walk in his ways, to keep his statutes, and his commandments, and his judgments, and his testimonies, as it is written in the law of Moses, that thou mayest prosper in all that thou doest, and whithersoever thou turnest thyself:

That the Lord may continue his word which he spake concerning me, saying, If thy children take heed to their way, to walk before me in truth with all their heart and with all their soul, there shall not fail thee (said he) a man on the throne of Israel.

The ancient city of Salem is near the location of modern Jeru**salem**. Look forward to more maps in the future!

1 Chronicles 29:23-25, KJV

Then Solomon sat on the throne of the Lord as king instead of David his father, and prospered; and all Israel obeyed him.

And all the princes, and the mighty men, and all the sons likewise of king David, submitted themselves unto Solomon the king.

And the Lord magnified Solomon exceedingly in the sight of all Israel, and bestowed upon him such royal majesty as had not been on any king before him in Israel.

1 Kings 4:21, 24-25, KJV

And Solomon reigned over all kingdoms from the river unto the land of the Philistines, and unto the border of Egypt: they brought presents, and served Solomon all the days of his life.

For he had dominion over all the region on this side the river, from Tiphsah even to Azzah, over all the kings on this side the river: and he had peace on all sides round about him.

And Judah and Israel dwelt safely, every man under his vine and under his fig tree, from Dan even to Beer-sheba, all the days of Solomon.

The Israelites had long been promised this particular geographic location… the promise traces back to the time of Melchizedek.

Hebrews 7:1-2, KJV

For this Melchisedec, king of Salem, priest of the most high God, who met Abraham returning from the slaughter of the kings, and blessed him;

To whom also Abraham gave a tenth part of all; first being by interpretation King of righteousness, and after that also King of Salem, which is, King of peace;

Genesis 17:8, KJV

And I will give unto thee, and to thy seed after thee, the land wherein thou art a stranger, all the land of Canaan, for an everlasting possession; and I will be their God.

Canaan is one of the names the land was called before it was called Israel.

Exodus 13:5, KJV

And it shall be when the Lord shall bring thee into the land of the Canaanites, and the Hittites, and the Amorites, and the Hivites, and the Jebusites, which he sware unto thy fathers to give thee, a land flowing with milk and honey, that thou shalt keep this service in this month.

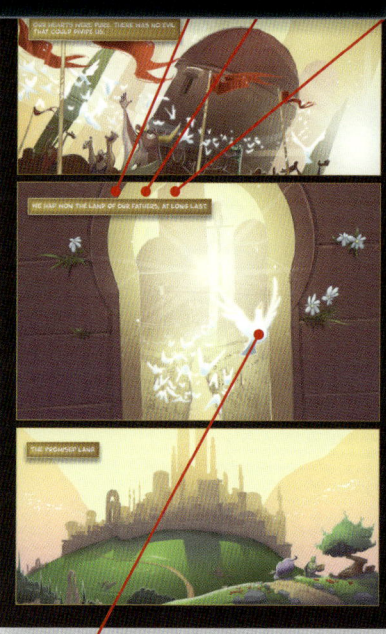

The Lord compared people that would one day visit Jerusalem (because of her splendor) to a cloud of doves.

Isaiah 60:8, KJV

Who are these that fly as a cloud, and as the doves to their windows?

Father/Son relationships (and family relationships in general) are at the heart of the Old Testament and the Book of Mormon, and as such they will be the "heart" of From the Dust as well.

Inspired by African Softshell Turtles. They live in parts of Israel. A humble creature, to say the least.

Many people think of Israel as a desert. This is only partially true. Much of Israel is covered with beautiful grass and flowers in the spring...hence the land being a land of "milk and honey." Bees have lots of flowers to pollinate and cows and goats have lots of grass to eat. Mmm...delicious! Not to mention beautiful! Look up some photos of Galilee in the spring and you will see entire fields carpeted with flowers.

Expect these things to disappear as the people of Israel choose to pollute and abuse their land of promise by defiling it with sin.

Notice the doves are flying away, never to return...except in the last days.

Deuteronomy 30:1, 16-20, KJV

And it shall come to pass, when all these things are come upon thee, the blessing and the curse, which I have set before thee, and thou shalt call them to mind among all the nations, whither the Lord thy God hath driven thee.

In that I command thee this day to love the Lord thy God, to walk in his ways, and to keep his commandments and his statutes and his judgments, that thou mayest live and multiply: and the Lord thy God shall bless thee in the land whither thou goest to possess it.

But if thine heart turn away, so that thou wilt not hear, but shalt be drawn away, and worship other gods, and serve them;

I denounce unto you this day, that ye shall surely perish, and that ye shall not prolong your days upon the land, whither thou passest over Jordan to go to possess it.

I call heaven and earth to record this day against you, that I have set before you life and death, blessing and cursing: therefore choose life, that both thou and thy seed may live:

That thou mayest love the Lord thy God, and that thou mayest obey his voice, and that thou mayest cleave unto him: for he is thy life, and the length of thy days: that thou mayest dwell in the land which the Lord sware unto thy fathers, to Abraham, to Isaac, and to Jacob, to give them.

Moses delineated many curses if the people should break their covenants. See Deuteronomy 28-30.

One of the curses got put in Chapter 1! Check out the following:

Deuteronomy 28:31, KJV

Thine ass shall be violently taken away from before thy face, and shall not be restored to thee...

Speaking of Israel's spiritual fall, Isaiah said:

Isaiah 64:6, KJV

But we are all as an unclean thing, and all our righteousnesses are as filthy rags; and we all do fade as a leaf; and our iniquities, like the wind, have taken us away.

Alma 37:28, BoM

For behold, there is a curse upon all this land, that destruction shall come upon all those workers of darkness, according to the power of God, when they are fully ripe; therefore I desire that this people might not be destroyed.

Israel wasn't the only land with a promise and a curse. The Americas (and all nations) have this same promise. It was less a promise on the land as it was on the people who lived on the land. The following scripture clarifies this idea:

Enos 1:10, BoM

And while I was thus struggling in the spirit, behold, the voice of the Lord came into my mind again, saying: I will visit thy brethren according to their diligence in keeping my commandments. I have given unto them this land, and it is a holy land; and I curse it not save it be for the cause of iniquity; wherefore, I will visit thy brethren according as I have said; and their transgressions will I bring down with sorrow upon their own heads.

Jeremiah 9:11, KJV

And I will make Jerusalem heaps, and a den of dragons; and I will make the cities of Judah desolate, without an inhabitant.

Wait…did you say…dragons?

Over 1000 years before the Babylonian invasion, Moses prophesied the day would come that Israel would fall if she did not fulfill her part of the covenant…

Notice the sun is setting…it will not rise again on Israel until the last days…if you were expecting From the Dust *to be a cheery, happy, picture-perfect story… you probably haven't read your scriptures much lately.*

Deuteronomy 28:49-50, KJV

The Lord shall bring a nation against thee from far, from the end of the earth, as swift as the eagle flieth; a nation whose tongue thou shalt not understand; A nation of fierce countenance…

Chaldeans = Babylonians.

Pronounced like it starts with a K. "Kaldeans." Like the Old Testament, From the Dust *sometimes interchanges the words Chaldeans and Babylonians. Babylon and Chaldea were neighboring city-states that were both part of the Babylonian Empire.*

Jeremiah 51:34, KJV

Nebuchadrezzar the king of Babylon hath devoured me, he hath crushed me, he hath made me an empty vessel, he hath swallowed me up like a dragon, he hath filled his belly with my delicates, he hath cast me out.

This scripture is one of the verses that was the first inspiration for From the Dust.

The King's Palace, also called the King's House, was built by Solomon at the time of his reign. This palace was largely built and decorated with wood, specifically, the famous cedars of Lebanon. Most people do not think of wood when they think of Jerusalem, but read for yourself!

1 Kings 7:1-5, KJV

But Solomon was building his own house thirteen years, and he finished all his house. He built also the house of the forest of Lebanon; the length thereof was an hundred cubits, and the breadth thereof fifty cubits, and the height thereof thirty cubits, upon four rows of cedar pillars, with cedar beams upon the pillars. And it was covered with cedar above upon the beams, that lay on forty five pillars, fifteen in a row. And there were windows in three rows, and light was against light in three ranks. And all the doors and posts were square, with the windows: and light was against light in three ranks.

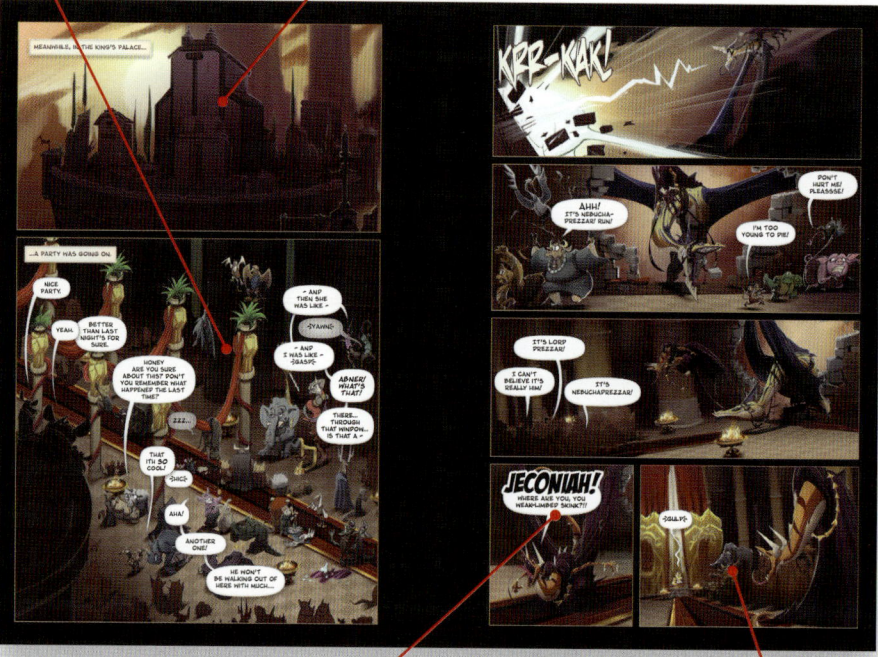

A skink is a lizard that lives in Israel. There are many different types of skinks in this world but every last one of them is weak-limbed!

The loyalty of Jeconiah's followers is about as deep as their spirituality. Contrast this loyalty with that which our main characters will develop on their epic journey.

> **Genesis 49:10, KJV**
>
> The sceptre shall not depart from Judah, nor a lawgiver from between his feet, until Shiloh come; and unto him shall the gathering of the people be.

A scepter for ancient Israelites symbolized the right of a king to rule. In modern times we usually give kings a crown on their head for the same reason. In the above scripture most people interpret Shiloh as the Messiah. We will be coming back to this scripture in the future. It's deep.

Technically, it was Jeconiah's father Jehoiakim that made an alliance with Pharaoh of Egypt, not Jeconiah. In this instance we have composited Jeconiah and his father into a single character. Don't worry if things are confusing right now and all these names are hard to remember - it will all become clearer in the future as you meet these characters in the storyline!

You are beginning to see why Babylon came to symbolize the evil things of the world. even today we sing:

"O Babylon, O Babylon, we bid thee farewell / we're going to the Mountains of Ephraim to dwell." (Hymn 319, Ye Elders of Israel)

Zedekiah is a blind mole rat. why a mole rat as the last king of Judah? Two reasons:

1) He actually gets his eyes put out later in the story, so he kind of becomes the "creation myth" for blind mole rats. (Don't worry, mom, it won't be graphic!)

2) He has lots of kids (like rodents), one of whom survives (Mulek) and makes it into our Book of Mormon storyline (the Mulekites.)

> **2 Kings 25:7, KJV**
>
> And they slew the sons of Zedekiah before his eyes, and put out the eyes of Zedekiah, and bound him with fetters of brass, and carried him to Babylon.

2 Kings 24:17-19, KJV

And the king of Babylon made Mattaniah his father's brother king in his stead, and changed his name to Zedekiah.

Zedekiah was twenty and one years old when he began to reign, and he reigned eleven years in Jerusalem. And he did that which was evil in the sight of the Lord, according to all that Jehoiakim had done.

Yes! It's for real! You had been warned over 100 years earlier that this would happen…if you'd only read your scriptures!

Isaiah 3:1-4, KJV

For, behold, the Lord, the Lord of hosts, doth take away from Jerusalem and from Judah the stay and the staff, the whole stay of bread, and the whole stay of water, the mighty man, and the man of war, the judge, and the prophet, and the prudent, and the ancient, the captain of fifty, and the honourable man, and the counsellor, and the cunning artificer, and the eloquent orator.

And I will give children to be their princes, and babes shall rule over them.

Few readers of the Book of Mormon realize that Zedekiah was a weak puppet-king to Nebuchadrezzar. Nephi introduces his record with this simple sentence:

1 Nephi 1:4, BoM

For it came to pass in the commencement of the first year of the reign of Zedekiah, King of Judah…

What he is really saying is "In the first year of the weak puppet-king Zedekiah, his predecessors being a long line of equally weak leaders…a time when many of our best people were exiled to Babylon and when many false prophets roamed the land…our story begins."

While we don't know the exact details of these events (the double tribute part is made up), we do know the following about Nebuchadrezzar's (sometimes called Nebuchadnezzar) visit to Jerusalem:

2 Kings 24:10-14, KJV

At that time the servants of Nebuchadnezzar king of Babylon came up against Jerusalem, and the city was besieged.

And Nebuchadnezzar king of Babylon came against the city, and his servants did besiege it.

And he carried away all Jerusalem, and all the princes, and all the mighty men of valour, even ten thousand captives, and all the craftsmen and smiths: none remained, save the poorest sort of the people of the land.

Jeconiah's deposition, which you just witnessed, is a little more complicated than From the Dust *makes it seem in this opening chapter. We'll tell the full story in the future. For now, just realize that all of the following also happened and it was a very trying time for Jerusalem.*

Quite literally "carried away." In some ways, by making the story a fantasy we are able to be more accurate to the Biblical text. Weird, huh?

2 Kings 24:15-16, KJV

And he carried away [Jeconiah] to Babylon, and the king's mother, and the king's wives, and his officers, and the mighty of the land, those carried he into captivity from Jerusalem to Babylon.

And all the men of might, even seven thousand, and craftsmen and smiths a thousand, all that were strong and apt for war, even them the king of Babylon brought captive to Babylon.

Hebrew

A Brief History of
The Language of the Scriptures.

" *My soul delights in reading the word of the Lord in the original.* "

— Joseph Smith

Genesis 1:1
(read right to left)

אלהים ברא בראשית
el-o-heem   bah-rah   bare-ray-sheet
God   created   in the beginning

את השמים ואת הארץ
ha-air-ets   vuh-et   ha-sha-ma-yeem   et
the earth   and   the heavens   —

What is the Hebrew Bible?

Let's consider this book called the Hebrew Bible. "The Hebrew Bible" is another way of saying "the Old Testament." The term is generally used by scholars, but it is also extensively used in *From the Dust*. We would recommend memorizing right now that "Hebrew Bible" is interchangeable with "Old Testament" and means "all the books from Genesis to Malachi."[1]

"The Hebrew Bible" is a wonderful name for the books of the Old Testament. The name emphasizes its authors' culture and language, as well as signifies that it is a collection of related books rather than a single book alone. The English word "bible" comes from Greek, *biblia*, which means "books." Simply put, "the Hebrew Bible" means "the Books of the Hebrews." And who were the Hebrews? They were descendents of Abraham, or Abraham's "family." The Hebrew Bible contains their poetry, their songs, their sacred writings, their law, and many personal accounts of historical events and divine

---

[1] Because some Christians have additional books in their Old Testament, the term "Hebrew Bible" is not *always* directly interchangeable with "the Old Testament," but in the case of Latter-day Saints it is.

manifestations. If we want to understand what it means to "be Hebrew" the Hebrew Bible is the perfect place to start.

Hebrew-Speaking Saints

One of the many things the prophet Joseph Smith did when he established the School of the Prophets was hire a Hebrew instructor. Over the course of the next several months he and many church leaders learned all they could about this unique and beautiful language.

There are many reasons to learn Hebrew, not the least of which is that it adds depth to our understanding of scriptural passages. Even passages that are very plain in English can take on powerful new meanings when considered from a Hebrew language perspective. It is not necessary to learn Hebrew fluently; an understanding of individual words can add substantially to your scriptural journey. Not only this, but many modern names find their origins in Hebrew, including Michael, David, and Rachel, to name just a few. Wouldn't it be cool to read your name in its *original* language?

History of Hebrew

Just like English has evolved substantially in the last few hundred years (ehver tryed tew reade Chaucer's Canterbury Tales?) So too did Hebrew evolve substantially over generations. It's important to understand this as the Hebrew that the Hebrew Bible was originally written in is quite different from the Hebrew that we read it in today.

Did you know?

Moses' first language was Egyptian. He is attributed with writing the first five books of the Old Testament.

Let's take a look at the three main divisions of Hebrew alphabets throughout history. They represent what little we know about how Hebrew evolved over time. For simplicity's sake, we have divided these three alphabets into Moses' Hebrew, Jeremiah's Hebrew, and Malachi's Hebrew.

Moses' Hebrew

Proto-Sinaitic

Moses' Hebrew isn't really Hebrew at all. It is called Proto-Sinaitic script. It means "First language of the Sinai Peninsula." It is thought that this script (which dates to the time of Moses) could be one of the links between Egyptian and Hebrew. It was discovered in the early 20th century and remains largely a mystery to scholars.

Moses, the writer of the first five books of the Hebrew Bible, didn't speak the Hebrew that we know today, or even the Hebrew that Jeremiah and Lehi in *From the Dust* would have known. He definitely spoke and wrote Egyptian languages, as he was raised as a prince of Egypt. While it is possible he may have originally written the first five books of the Hebrew Bible in Egyptian, the Hebrew University of Jerusalem identifies Proto-Sinaitic script as a predecessor to Hebrew.[2] If so, Moses may have used it. We don't know much about this language as less than 30 inscriptions exist. Some scholars feel the site where these inscriptions exist may be where Moses and the Israelites first made camp after the Exodus from Egypt. The facts are we don't know for certain what languages Moses originally wrote his prophecies in, but it was almost certainly different than those of future prophets as over 1000 years separated them.

---

[2] Not all scholars agree on this due to lack of conclusive evidence.

Jeremiah's Hebrew

Paleo-Hebrew

Jeremiah's Hebrew is called Paleo-Hebrew or Old Hebrew. This is what major parts of the Hebrew Bible were originally written in and it's what *From the Dust* characters (including Lehi) would have spoken in real life. Like Moses' Hebrew, this alphabet doesn't have a lot of archaeological evidences, but the handful of them that have been found will be highlighted in future issues of *From the Dust*. They include pottery shards from Lehi's day mentioning prophets, war, and danger; wall inscriptions in underground passageways, and also a few books of scriptures including parts of Genesis, Exodus, and Leviticus, as well as burial ornaments quoting scriptures and more. In addition, quite a few bullae, or personal seals, have been found (along with coins and things).

Like Proto-Sinaitic, Paleo-Hebrew is a relatively new and exciting discovery in just the last century. It is a real treasure! It helps us to understand the world of Jerusalem at the time of its destruction, and also gives us insights into how the Hebrew culture changed over time.

Malachi's Hebrew

Biblical Hebrew

Malachi was the last prophet of the Hebrew Bible. Malachi's Hebrew is called Biblical Hebrew, or sometimes Classical Hebrew or "block" script. This developed sometime in the 5th century BC, more than 100 years after the story of *From the Dust* ends. The Israelites in captivity borrowed the Aramaic alphabet used by their captors (at that time the Persian Empire, the Babylonian Empire had fallen). This is the alphabet we will be learning as it's the same one in use in Israel today, and the alphabet that most of the Hebrew manuscripts that currently exist are recorded in. (It's also the alphabet Joseph Smith learned.)

עזרת המזבח מטוב ואת חלט וקטור המזבח
חקרב ואת אשר על הקרבום ואת וותות הנבר

It's important to note that we don't know how much the Hebrew culture changed from Moses' time in 1700 BC down to Malachi in the 5th century BC when this block script was adopted, but if the alphabets are any sign of the cultures, these cultures may have been pretty different.

As you read *From the Dust*, you will find that Jeremiah struggles to preserve his Hebrew culture against a tide of people that are destroying it. This observation on the alphabets is just an observation, but it may be related to Jeremiah's struggles.

Biblical Hebrew has not changed significantly since Malachi's time, but Hebrew as a spoken language was replaced by Aramaic (which is possibly what Jesus of Nazareth spoke). Eventually the Hebrew language was relegated to Rabbinical purposes and ultimately died around AD 300.

For about 1500 years only scribes learned Hebrew. It had become a dead language, just like Latin.

Modern Hebrew

A dead language comes to life.

That's when this guy comes in: Eliezer Ben-Yehuda.

He was incredibly passionate about restoring his culture's identity, and as such he worked hard to bring about a revival of the spoken language of Hebrew, which miraculously he succeeded in doing. To our knowledge Hebrew is the only language that has been successfully artificially revived. Hebrew is now the national language of Israel and is spoken as their native tongue. This has not been the case for over 2000 years!

בְּרֵאשִׁית בָּרָא אֱלֹהִים אֵת הַשָּׁמַיִם וְאֵת הָאָרֶץ׃
וְהָאָרֶץ הָיְתָה תֹהוּ וָבֹהוּ וְחֹשֶׁךְ עַל־פְּנֵי תְהוֹם וְרוּחַ

If you go to Israel you will be able to use your Hebrew to get around town, but until then, you will be able to use it to better understand the amazing Hebrew heritage that we share with many of our brothers and sisters in many religions and cultures throughout the world!

Archaeology has not uncovered as much as you would think in terms of artifacts concerning the original languages of the Hebrew Bible, meaning Moses' Hebrew and Jeremiah's Hebrew. These languages have only recently been uncovered. In *From the Dust*'s educational sections we will be taking a look at many of these artifacts to help us understand these people's cultures and histories. For some cultures only one or two artifacts have *ever* been found. Others...*none*.

The origins of the Hebrew Bible are shrouded in mystery — what an exciting adventure we're on! By the end of it you will have a great respect for the people who wrote the Hebrew Bible, for their cultures, their stories, and the incredible sacrifices they made to give us this amazing treasure!

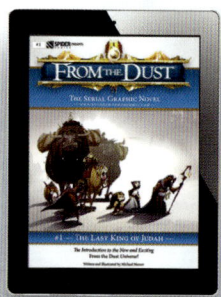

Sketchbook

Lesson #1

Drawing is a Language, not a Talent.

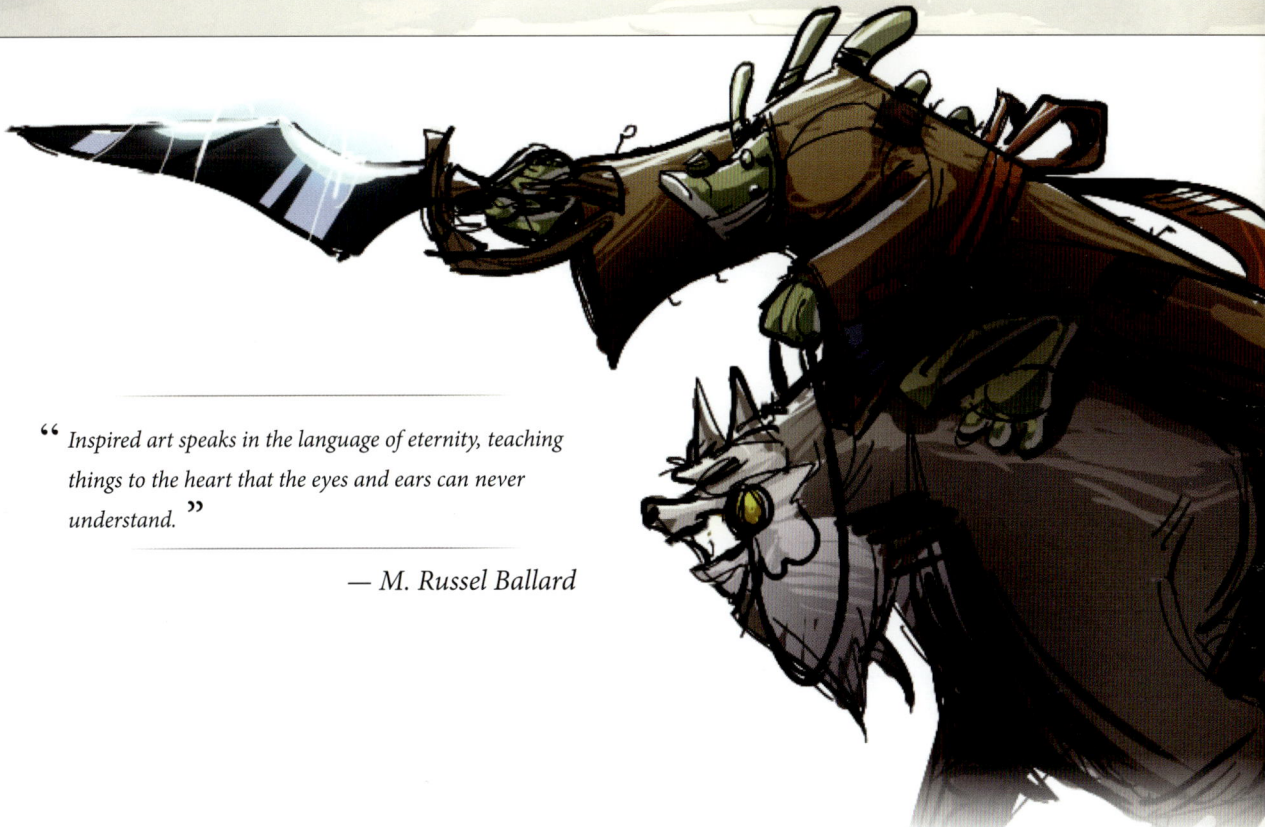

> *Inspired art speaks in the language of eternity, teaching things to the heart that the eyes and ears can never understand.*
>
> — M. Russel Ballard

Contrary to popular belief, drawing is a learnable skill just like math, English, or basketball. The problem with drawing is that most people don't understand how to identify their strengths and weaknesses, much less how to improve upon them or use them to benefit society in meaningful ways. In our sketchbook section you will get world-class tips on how to draw, how to make money drawing, how to use drawing to supplement many other careers (like programming and engineering), and how to use drawing to add richness and culture to your own life and to your community. In short, we will be teaching you how to appreciate and respect the visual world we live in every day. It is a beautiful and glorious place designed for us to enjoy! All the fundamental principles you need to appreciate sunsets, renaissance sculpture, and yes, even cartoons, are contained in the skill of drawing. First let's address the basic problems we face. Typically, the first problem is we *can't draw*.

How Not To Draw Like a 6-Year-Old

The answer to this is simple. Spend more time drawing! The chart below shows how much time most people spend drawing versus doing other activities.

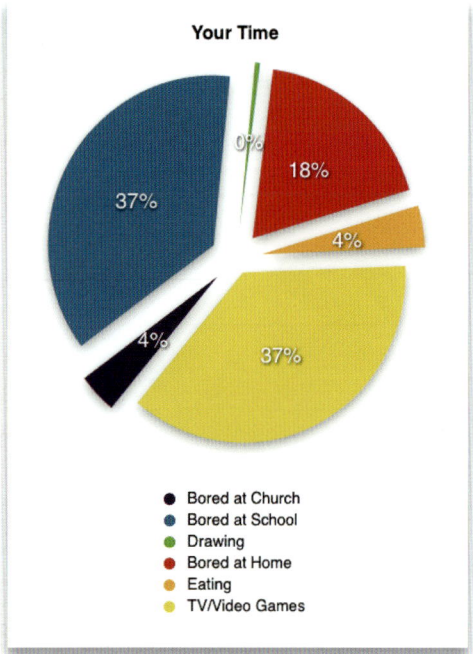

All of us start as cavemen scribbling out stick figures (so be patient with yourself). Luckily, you can get out of this stage quickly! The fastest way to learn to draw is to start devoting time and energy to it.

What to Draw

Drawings can generally be simplified to three types: drawings from life, master copies, and drawings from imagination. **Drawings from life** are anything that is in our real world that you sit down, observe, and then draw. **Master copies** are exact copies of any artist's work who is better than you. By copying them you absorb their superpowers. **Drawings from imagination** are anything you make up; they rely on skills and abilities learned from drawing from life and making master copies. Drawing from imagination is a more complex task. Start with drawing from life and making master copies and then build up to drawing from imagination.

The Secret is KISS

A popular motto in the art industry is KISS, Keep It Simple, Stupid. We tell ourselves this all the time! Keep your drawing hobby simple and stress-free. Start drawing what interests and appeals to you. Be sure to keep your morals straight and don't draw anything you can't show your friends or your parents. We're not Babylonians!

How to Draw

Start with the drawing tips on the next page. Then make observations about the sample scribbles that follow. Ask yourself:

- Which drawing is best? Why is it best?
- Why do I like this drawing? Why do I dislike it?
- If I had to draw [Lehi, Nephi, etc] right this instant (because your life depended on it)…how would I begin the drawing?
- What would I do first, then next?
- What is/isn't working in this drawing?
- How would I make this drawing better?

Then take these questions with you throughout your day and week and ask them often of everything you see in this beautiful world!

Then get the next issue of *From the Dust* and we'll give you another lesson!

DID YOU KNOW?

Many of the most "talented" artists throughout the ages started their training before their teenage years.

DRAWING TIPS

DO

- **Draw from your shoulder.** This helps you to draw circles and lines with greater precision.
- **Simplify characters into circles and tubes.** More on this in the future! Just dive in for now and start swimming!
- **Use cheap paper.** You're going to need a lot of it!
- **Copy your favorite artists.** It's not cheating, it's learning. Just liked copying letters in gradeschool taught you English, so will copying drawings teach you drawing.
- **Keep a regular sketchbook.** Show your sketchbook to your friends and give each other meaningful compliments. If possible, also help each other with kind critiques.
- **Talk about art.** Make observations about artwork and about the world around you. Keep your observations in your sketchbook.

DO NOT

- **Draw with your fingers.** We're not writing, we're drawing. Besides, even writing works better from the shoulder and wrist. Try it!
- **Let your fears stop you.** Learning takes courage. Be courageous!
- **Blame a bad drawing on your paper or pencil.** This is sissy and a lot of people do it. Don't be one of them!
- **Let a bad drawing make you feel like you can't draw.** Copy something. You'll feel better.
- **Draw the same things all the time.** It's like reading the same book over and over and over again. If you want to learn, draw something you've never drawn.
- **Rush!** It can sometimes be beneficial, but generally it inhibits learning.
- **Expect perfection!**

Ideas begin small, messy, quick, and usually in black and white.

Gesture   Pencil   Flat Color   Final

Jeremiah rides a runaway camel. See how messy it can get?

Laman studies.

Lehi drinks his morning wake-up juice. Don't worry, it's herbal.

A chameleon rider from Philistine.

Sariah frolics.

CONVERSATIONS
With Jeremiah
"Here There Be Dragons"

Panel 1: YOU KNOW THERE ARE DRAGONS IN THE BIBLE? / WHAT?!

Panel 2: WHAT DO YOU MEAN "WHAT" - YOU WROTE ABOUT IT YOURSELF! / NO I DIDN'T.

Panel 3: "AND I WILL MAKE JERUSALEM HEAPS, AND A DEN OF DRAGONS."

Panel 4: (silent)

Panel 5: ...WELL I DIDN'T MEAN IT LITERALLY!

Panel 6: ..YOU'RE NOT GOING TO PUT DRAGONS IN YOUR COMIC BOOK...ARE YOU?

Panel 7: YOU WANT ME TO TAKE THEM OUT...? BUT IT'S SO BORING ALREADY. NO ONE WOULD READ IT.

Panel 8: SORRY...JUST SAYIN'. / HEY!

Panel 9: I JUST THINK DRAGONS WOULD SPICE IT UP A BIT. / WELL, I DON'T THINK I WOULD LIKE IT.

Panel 10: WELL, YOU DON'T HAVE TO LIKE IT -

Panel 11: - YOU JUST HAVE TO NOT GET EATEN BY ONE.

Panel 12: THANKS A LOT.

Panel 13: WOOOOOOOO! AND **GIANTS** TOO!

Panel 14: I WONDER IF I CAN FIT IN THE TALKING DONKEY? / FWAP!

Panel 15: OH WAIT, THAT'S ALREADY BEEN DONE.

Panel 16: STUPID **SHREK!**

NEXT ISSUE

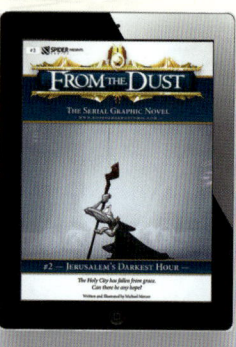

From the Dust #2
JERUSALEM'S DARKEST HOUR

WHAT'S INSIDE

- The **next chapter** of *From the Dust*!
- Over **30 pages** of full-color **story**!
- **Meet Jeremiah**, Lehi, Sariah, and **Nephi**!
- Experience **fallen Jerusalem**, the world our **heroes** live in!
- Plus **supplementary** education and **art** material!

PLEASE ENJOY THE FOLLOWING 2-PAGE EXCERPT!

WWW.BOOKOFMORMONCOMIC.COM

COMING **SOON.**

-SIGH-

WHERE IS ALL THAT NOISE COMING FROM?

YOU'VE GOT TO BE KIDDING ME!? ANOTHER ONE?!

IN MY LIFETIME I HAD WITNESSED THE COMPLETE DEGENERATION OF CIVILITY IN MY SOCIETY.

SELFISHNESS AND GREED WERE AROUND EVERY CORN-

DON'T MISS FROM THE DUST #2: JERUSALEM'S DARKEST HOUR WITH OVER 30 PAGES OF STORY!

Sneak Peek

An Insider's Look
at From the Dust #3: Nephi's First Hunt

> "I will also send wild beasts among you, which shall rob you of your children, and destroy your cattle, and make you few in number; and your high ways shall be desolate."
>
> — Leviticus 26:22

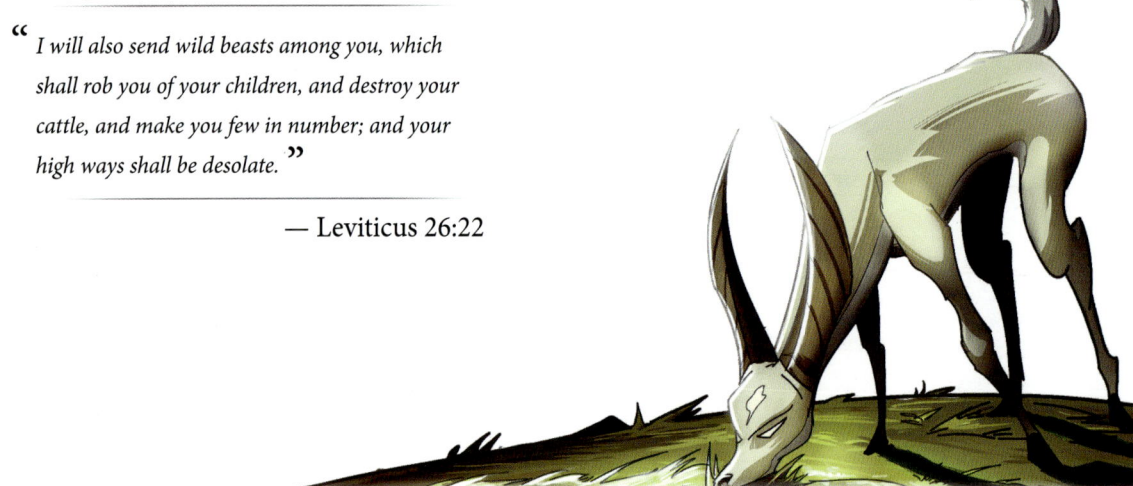

In *From the Dust #3: Nephi's First Hunt*, we meet the Sons of Lehi: Laman, Lemuel, Sam, and Nephi. The Sons of Lehi are well known for their myriad talents and abilities, not the least of which is hunting. Lehi has taught them well, and he expects excellence from them in every field. They do not disappoint. Although still teenagers, Laman (19-years-old) and Lemuel (18-years-old) can outperform, outlast, and outwit (well, maybe not Lemuel…) most anyone at anything. They are physically impressive… and intimidating. Laman and Lemuel are rarely separated, but you won't see Sam (15-years-old) tagging along with them. He's just not quite cool enough to hang out with his older brothers.

One exception to this is hunting, where Lehi has mandated his sons learn to work together as a team. Hunting season is Sam's time to truly prove himself…useless. It's true, unfortunately. Sam isn't very good at hunting, or much else, at least when compared with his amazing brothers. Showing kindness to his younger siblings, and people in general, is one of Sam's many under-valued virtues. Sam convinces his father to let his younger brother Nephi (12-years-old) come on the hunt this year. His reasons are two-fold. First, he feels Nephi would love the experience and be good at it, and second, he doesn't want to be the only one to screw things up this time around. But Sam doesn't realize that little Nephi has an incredible destiny all his own…

Chapter 3

Nephi's First Hunt

The Judean Highlands, a world of ruins. It is the promised land of the Tribe of Judah.

Twenty generations of my people, the Israelites, have lived here. This land was old when my people arrived 1000 years ago. Many thousands of years of other empires have built their fortresses in these mountains. They have all since been destroyed. The sun has set on them...just as it is setting on us. It is only a matter of time now, before we, too, shall be blown to the wind. My people are weakening, and all that will be left of us is stone and crumbling mortar, like those that have come before...

15 MINUTES LATER...

"ALRIGHT. WE'RE IN POSITION."

"SAM, TAKE THE SPEAR."

"NOW ALL YOU HAVE TO DO IS TAKE THE POINTY END AND JAB IT INTO ONE OF THEM. RIGHT?"

"AND NEPHI YOU GET MY KNIFE SINCE YOU'RE TOO SMALL TO WIELD A BOW."

"YOUR KNIFE!? WHOA, WAIT A MINUTE, HERE. NEPHI'S NOT BIG ENOUGH TO —"

"I CAN DO THIS."

BIOGRAPHY

MICHAEL MERCER
Writer & Illustrator of From the Dust

> " *Like my father before me and his father before him, I'm a mechanic. Rather than cars, however, I fix stories. I guess the drive to fix things is in my blood.* "
>
> — Mike

Michael was born in the rural mountain valleys of the Black Hills of South Dakota. His family moved when he was a child to the suburbs of Atlanta, Georgia, where he was raised.

At age 19 he served a full-time mission for the Church of Jesus Christ of Latter-day Saints. He spent two years with the loving and kind people of the Philippine islands.

He graduated with a BFA in Animation from Brigham Young University in 2009. Michael has since worked in the social gaming industry and comic book industry. Michael's dream has always been to serve valuable social needs with his artwork. As such, in 2011 he began working on *From the Dust*, a high-quality family entertainment property for the Latter-day Saint market.

He loves to social dance, especially West Coast Swing. He also enjoys the outdoors: climbing, hiking, and running.